PRAYER-talk

PRAYER-talk

casual conversations with God

William V.
Coleman

AVE MARIA PRESS Notre Dame, Indiana

International Standard Book Number: 0-87793-265-4

Library of Congress Catalog Card Number: 82-74085

Printed and bound in the United States of America.

Cover and text design: Carol A. Robak

Photography:
    pg. 17, Religious News Service
    pg. 29, Rohn Engh
    pg. 44, Diane M. Bellavia
    pg. 56, John David Arms
    pg. 86, James Shaffer
    pg. 101, Paul M. Schrock

To Patty, my own image of God

Contents

Introduction

This book was written for people who are uncertain they know how to pray. They are neither saints nor sinners, just ordinary people who would like to raise their minds and hearts to God. Much of what holds them back from prayer is fear. They imagine that prayer requires a blameless life or, at least, a mind trained in the intricacies of meditation and the spiritual life.

Yet, the people Jesus taught to pray were simple people. They were not perfect men or women, nor were they schooled in intricate ways of prayer. He urged them to pray simply, to talk to God as Father, and to praise, thank, ask and seek forgiveness as they prayed.

Perhaps the reason so many of us are afraid of prayer is that we remember childhood stories of saintly people who climbed inside trees to pray or lived in the desert in order to forge a relationship with God. We fear a prayer life that will require such behavior of us.

Then, too, many of us were taught such reverence for God that we still get tongue-tied when we try to speak to him. He has been called the "absolute Other," and how can we learn to speak to someone who has no understanding of our petty experiences and feelings? What is so often missing in our understanding of prayer is that the great God is our own Father, and that he chose to share all the uncertainty of human life.

My first breakthrough, if you can call it that, in this business of prayer came the night I saw the play, *Fiddler On the Roof*. I immediately identified with the leading character, Tevye. He was my kind of person, so strong and yet so docile, so sure of the Law and yet so ready to let his love make exceptions to it. Between the scenes of the play Tevye spoke to God. We in the audience never heard God's voice, but I was sure he was there dialoging with Tevye, stretching Tevye's mind and calling his certainties into question.

I began to ask myself, Why not pray as Tevye did? No reason at all, really. All that was needed was a sense of humor and an ability to talk to God as frankly as I would to my own father. In time I learned that Tevye's kind of prayer was in an old rabbinic tradition, a tradition with roots so old that Jesus himself might well have prayed that way.

The meditations in this book always begin with Tevye-like conversation with God. I hope that some of the humor of life finds its way into the conversations and that the immense good sense of God prevails. Some have asked why these conversations always begin with God's voice. The answer is simple enough and quite humbling. All our prayer is at God's prompting. Even when we think we began a prayer, God took the first step without our even noticing it.

These conversations are followed by another form of prayer I have come to treasure—the story. Stories are simple narratives that say just enough to start me thinking and dialoging with God on my own. This was the way Jesus taught, of course. Truth is contained in the story, but it is never so obvious that it stills the inquisitive mind. Meditating on stories leads to all sorts of alleys, some blind and some opening to whole new understandings of reality.

Then, I have chosen a reflection that tries to make sense of modern life and traditional cautions. Because truth, although ever the same, cannot be frozen in language that is immobile, reflections on our modern life are quite essential if we are to keep in touch with both our roots and our present reality.

Finally, each meditation ends with a poetic summary of all that has gone before. Poems have a way of expressing not only what is in our minds, but what our hearts wish to speak.

These are the kinds of prayer you will find in this book, all prayer forms that can lead you into a deeper, fuller friendship with God. If these meditations move you to talk to God or even smile with him, they will have done their task.

—William V. Coleman

Prayer-talk

Creativity

God: Did I hear you say you were tired, bored and a little bit depressed?

Me: Well, yes, God, I did say that. Sometimes I feel burned out. All my dreams have turned to ashes and I wonder what this life you have given me is all about.

God: Ah, so that's it. You heard that new term, *burned out*, and like so many other diseases, you imagine you have it too. How can you be burned out when the whole world needs you so much?

Me: Needs me? You have to be kidding. The real trouble is that no one seems to want me. I teach and lead and no one listens or follows. I'm terribly tired.

God: What you are is not tired but discouraged. You have lost your courage to be creative. That's what the trouble is.

Me: As usual, God, you are right. I have lost my courage to be creative. But, is that a sin? Is it wrong to want to hide a little while and nurse my wounds?

God: I made you in my own image and likeness. Remember, I am the Creator. Part of being like me is creating, all day, every day.

Me: But, God, I'm so tired, so burned out.

God: No time for all that. You and I have too much to do together. We have a whole world to attend to. We are needed out there.

Me: If you will be with me, God, perhaps then . . .

God: I am always with you. Bundle up your fears and come along with me. The best is yet to be.

____A Story____

Once upon a time, an old man sat in front of his fireplace gazing at the ashes. He imagined that he, like the ashes, was useless, all his fire gone.

When he scooped up the ashes to throw them outside, some of them fell into an open vat of warm lard. The old man was so discouraged with himself that he left the ashes where they fell.

The next morning he trudged into the kitchen to clean up the mess and discovered, not lard and ashes, but soap.

Even burned out ashes have a purpose when used creatively. How much more we, who are made in the image and likeness of God, the Creator.

____Reflection____

The past century has brought a quiet but profound revolution. Less than 100 years ago Sigmund Freud was making exciting discoveries about the subconscious. Fifty years ago Christians generally ignored their feelings or sought to bring them under the control of reason. Twenty years ago Catholic people opened the Vatican II window and in flew much new thought about the subconscious and about feelings.

It has been a good thing, of course. Yet, like all good things, feelings can be taken much too seriously. We can come to believe that we have no control over our emotions, that they rule our lives.

Perhaps the very beginning of creativity is gaining control of our own lives, the vast void that Genesis speaks about. We can and must take complete charge of our lives, including our emotions. Once integrated, these powerful urges can lend our personalities and our work warmth, sensitivity and full beauty.

Left to themselves, however, feelings can turn into moods and moodiness. They may snuff out all desire to serve others and, with that desire, any truly Christian spirit.

____*Prayer*____

Lord, God, Creator of us all,
    you made us body and spirit,
    beautiful to the deepest core.
    in your image you created us
    and set us over all of your creation.

Now, I am tired of creating,
    discouraged perhaps,
    burned out, some say.

I want to go away
    and hide my creative gifts
    because others have not loved them
    and me who created just for them.

Encourage me, Lord,
    fill my heart with fire
    and the enthusiasm to begin again
    to create new ways, new designs,
    new words, new programs,
    and, especially, a new me.

Amen, Lord. Amen.

Passion

God: What I need is passionate people!

Me: But, God, passionate people? Isn't that a little strong? Aren't we supposed to be moderate in all things?

God: Of course moderation is necessary. But there must be passion to be moderated. Today all I hear about is moderation; passion has been left behind.

Me: Do you mean you approve of demonstrators and activists?

God: You have to admit they have fire in their veins. They make mistakes like the rest of my children, but they do care deeply. In caring, they are like my son, Jesus.

Me: But, God, they are involved in politics. They sometimes break the law and, who knows, may even be in conflict with religious authorities.

God: I know, I know. Yet they *are* passionate. After all, Jesus was involved with politics, broke the law, and even entered into conflict with the religious leaders of his time. He was anything but cautious.

Me: Do you want me to act like that?

God: I want you to be passionate, full of concern. I want you to love so powerfully that you forget about yourself and take risks for what you love. Then you will be like my son, Jesus.

____*A Story*____

The young teacher was cautious. He knew how to look out for Number One. Never did he say the wrong word, appear with the wrong people, stay too long in the wrong job. Everyone predicted for him a future marked by financial and professional success.

Some said the young professor was calculating. In a way he was. He never married, but did keep a mistress. The idea of a commitment, a passionate love, did not fit in with his plans for success. No impediments, please!

One day the teacher had a remarkable experience, an awakening in which he discovered Jesus. For Augustine, life was never the same. Passion overwhelmed him and he became a most remarkable Christian saint.

____*Reflection*____

Sociologists tell us that the mark of modern civilization is bureaucracy. Russian communism is a bureaucracy. American corporations are bureaucratic. Government, industry, medicine, education, and even religion are all bureaucratic, in part at least. In itself a bureaucracy is neither good nor bad. Yet it has within it the power to drug the human spirit.

Bureaucracies demand that people do things *not well but correctly*. They make their subjects law-abiding, which is good, but tend to sap passion and concern for anything but correctness. Teachers worry about reports rather than children. Physicians worry about insurance forms rather than cures. Priests worry about setting up the right committees rather than preaching exciting homilies. Form becomes more important than content.

Living in a bureaucratic world, and all of us must, carries with it the danger of dampening, even killing, our passion. We can so easily become immoderately moderate.

_____*Prayer*_____

Lord,
    have I become like Gulliver,
    bound by a thousand tiny ropes
    of convention and formality?

Have I forgotten the excitement
    of fast-flowing blood in my veins,
    of sweaty palms
    and a heart that beats
    in a wild, unmeasured cadence?

Help me recapture passion in my life,
    the desire to do and feel and love
    even at the risk of seeming
    foolish, immoderate and fanatic.

May I understand that the only limit
    to love
    is to love without limit—
    as you do.

Amen.

Loyalty

God: Did I tell you how much I enjoy the Boy Scout Law?

Me: But, God, that is for children. We adults have to look for something a little less concrete, something more in keeping with our own moral development. You've kept up with modern psychology, haven't you?

God: Oh yes. And some of the ideas are good, very good indeed. But let's return to the Boy Scout Law and its second word, *loyal*. I think loyalty is a virtue you should consider very seriously.

Me: Ah, loyalty. Good virtue, certainly, but loyalty to whom? That's the question, isn't it?

God: Yes, it is. Let's begin with loyalty to family, to parents, to children, to brothers and sisters.

Me: And can't we add loyalty to the government and to the church?

God: Sure, provided you remember that all loyalty to people and institutions must be balanced by a loyalty to me. Loyalty to me was Moses' first commandment. It is still the heart of a holy life.

Me: Yes, loyalty to you, God. But what does that mean?

God: It means that I come first—before family, before government, before church. As my son, Jesus, put it, "He who loves father or mother more than me is not worthy of me." The same goes for all institutions, even the most sacred.

_____*A Story*_____

His bishop told him that his first obligation was to his family. Government officials demanded that he either enlist in the army or face prison and death. Church and state, family and friends, demanded that he become a soldier.

Yet the young father of two beautiful little girls refused. He was carted off to jail and, in due time, executed. His wife became a widow, his children fatherless. The government branded him a traitor while church officials thought him a little touched.

Today, Franz Jagerstatter's refusal to help the Nazi war machine is regarded as an act of saintly heroism. Is it possible that Franz's counterparts are among us today, quietly loyal to a vision of God most of us have missed completely?

_____*Reflection*_____

Dr. Lawrence Kohlberg and other psychologists have researched and begun to chart human growth in moral decision-making. Kohlberg has even arranged our growth into six stages.

Without endorsing all of his work, we can glimpse in these stages an undisputed truth. We tend to move from the *individual* to the *universal* as we grow older and wiser. In the beginning our loyalty is to individuals, no more. As we grow that loyalty extends to rules, laws, principles and perhaps ends where it began—in unflinching loyalty to God, someone beyond all human laws and principles.

Loyalty to God marks the saint. He or she hears a voice and follows it. In spite of mistakes—and saints do make them—the saint shows an unswerving loyalty to God, admirable but perhaps a little frightening to the rest of us.

_____*Prayer*_____

Lord, God,
> I have not yet put my life together.
> I hear many voices, not a single one.
> I dance to a hundred rhythms
> and sing so many discordant songs.

May I somehow catch the single rhythm
    and hear the universal song
    you sing for me to hear.

May I bring my life toward a new
    loyalty, not to things or people,
    or institutions or even principles,
    but to you. Then, I shall be truly wise.

Help me, Lord. Amen.

Patience

God: I love a little bit of indignation. I will never forget the day my son, Jesus, drove the buyers and sellers out of the Temple. The way he wielded that whip, the fire in his eyes, the anger in his voice . . . I still smile when I think of it.

Me: That's something which has always puzzled me, God. I know patience is a gift of the Holy Spirit, and yet Jesus acted impatiently. There must be something I don't understand.

God: Yes, I can see your difficulty. You should be patient with people's foolishness, stupidity, insensitivity, and all the other ways they show their immaturity. But when the powerless are clearly being victimized, then I expect a little indignation and anger.

Me: Do you mean that I must let people victimize me but not others?

God: No, not really. I'm not promoting that at all. You must correct others when they need correcting. You do it for them as well as for the injured and innocent people.

Me: And then I sit patiently and wait for the results?

God: You're getting close. As long as you are concerned about others, the powerless who are being victimized and the powerful who are victims of their own desires, then you can correct with a good bit of indignation. Just be careful that you do not use the example of Jesus in the Temple to release your own bitterness and frustration.

Me: Being patient, then, God, is not an absolute at all, is it?

God: No virtue is without its limits except love. You are to love without limit as I do.

____ *A Story* ____

Every night as she climbed into bed beside her husband the middle-aged woman would say wearily, "I wish you would stop drinking. It is destroying our life together."

Every night her husband railed against her words. Some nights he became angry enough to hit her. Other nights he refused to speak. Sometimes he argued with her. Still, every night the woman delivered her message.

One day, for reasons she never understood, her husband did stop drinking. Now she says every night, "I am so proud of you. What you did took courage."

He invariably smiles and says, "It's easy to have courage when you have such a stubbornly patient wife."

____ *Reflection* ____

The Swiss psychiatrist, Carl Jung, says that all of us have two sides to our personalities, like two sides of a coin. On the one hand, we want to be aggressive and heroic. On the other hand, we enjoy being passive and the victim of others' aggressions. When both sides of our personality are in perfect balance, we are fully mature people.

Patience is usually understood as cultivating the victim (passive) side of our personality. It is this, of course, but it is more. True patience also has an aggressive edge to it. There are times and circumstances when the truly patient person challenges the evil round about.

To be totally passive is not to be patient. It is being a masochist, one who enjoys being a victim. To be totally aggressive is not to be heroic. It is being a sadist, one who enjoys inflicting pain on others. Both sides of the coin, both components of our personality, must develop hand in hand and strive toward balance.

____*Prayer*____

God, my Father,
>You are both gentle and stern.
>You can smile and frown.
>You know anger and can be at peace.
>You are a mystery to me.

I want control of everything in life
>or I want to run and hide from it.
>I am strong and purposeful one minute
>and weak and vacillating the next.

Lord, grant me the true spirit of patience,
>a patience which challenges evil
>in others and in myself,
>but knows that for all its feistiness
>it will never lose its peace.

Amen, God. Amen.

Joy

God: I was musing about Christians and how easily they forget the message of my son, Jesus.

Me: I agree, God. Obligation, commitment, duty, sacrifice—all things we tend to forget. We want to make Christianity soft and easy.

God: True, true, but that was not what I had in mind. I was thinking about joy. Joy is, if you remember, one of the fruits of the Spirit. That means that if you are full of joy, the Spirit is dwelling within you.

Me: But, God, we have so little time for joy. We have the problems of the world, the pressures of our families, the task of liberation, the renewal of the church. Every day we must face pressing problems.

God: Yes, you must and so must I. But in heaven we somehow manage joy. You tend to overlook it and even to suspect its simple smile.

Me: Do you mean we should be less concerned, less ambitious for what is good, less concerned about our suffering neighbor?

God: Not at all. But you could remember that your struggle is never totally successful. The world is never completely converted. Relax and remember that after all is said and done, the world is in my hands. I am responsible for it.

Me: And when I relax, God, I feel joy?

God: Right, and then you know that what you do is done for me and
with me and my Spirit lives within you.

_____ *A Story* _____

Some said she was a simple woman. Others were angered by her
composure and eternal smile. Those who knew her laughed at the idea
of her being simple and smiled to themselves at the trouble this woman's
composure caused fanatics on her left and right.

Some of these fanatics resented the woman so deeply that they
trumped up charges against her and cast her into jail. In time, she was
executed.

After her execution . . . well, that's another story. This woman
was Jesus come again, once more misunderstood, rejected, imprisoned
and put to death. What happened once is repeated time and time again.

_____ *Reflection* _____

Even good people can become fanatics. They may champion the best
of causes—the right to life, the position of women in society, the
liberty of the oppressed, the rights of the poor.

The problem with fanatics, however, is that they have forgotten
how to laugh. They take upon themselves some of the world's burdens
and narrowly focus their attention on carrying them. In the process of
becoming committed and concerned they forget that they are no more
than instruments in the hands of God.

At root, no matter how they deny it, fanatics are atheists. They
live as if the world depended on them and not on God. They never
smile, never laugh, never relax, never know the smile of God within
their hearts.

Joy is the signature of the Holy Spirit. When joy is absent, the
Spirit is too.

——*Prayer*——

Lord, you are a smiling God.
>Your love never obscures your joy.
>You are never so concerned you cannot laugh
>and enjoy the beauty of the world you have created.

You share our concerns,
>our desires and determinations,
>but you know when to put them down
>and let a smile relax your face.

You smile at little children's innocence,
>at adolescents' awakening selves,
>at adults and their worrisome anxieties,
>at sin's foolishness
>and even at our bumbling attempts to end all evil.

You are a joyful God.
>Let that joy be reflected on our faces
>now and forever.

Amen.

Strength

God: Did you know that my greatest strength is in my weakness?

Me: Let me try that on again, God. Your greatest strength is in your weakness. How can that be?

God: It's true of you, too, or didn't you know? Your greatest strength is in your weakness.

Me: No, God, I didn't know, and I am not at all sure I know right now. Is this one of those mysteries we will understand only when we get to heaven?

God: Oh, no. This is something you must understand now so that you can live the kind of life my son, Jesus, recommended so highly. His strength, too, was in his weakness. You see, he was so strong he could afford to allow others to imagine that he was weak. He did not have to impress them with his strength because he knew it was there.

Me: Are you saying that when we try to show others how strong we are, this is a sign that inside we are really weak or at least fear that we are?

God: Precisely. The more you act strong, the more sure I am (most people are, too, by the way) that you are really weak. Did you ever notice a child making a muscle? What did you do?

Me: I had to smile.

God: Why?

Me: Because I knew he wasn't very strong, so making a muscle was just a bit funny.

God: How often world leaders, primates and princes, presidents and plutocrats make their little muscles. The really strong men and women need no pretense. Like me, they are content to appear weak.

____ A Story ____

Once there was a very fancy tailor shop in New York's finest fashion district. Into this shop came doctors, lawyers, executives, university presidents, and all the great of the world. The tailors were the aristocrats of their trade, the fabrics among the world's finest, and the salespeople proud of both their clients and their wares.

One day a small, bedraggled, white-haired man came into the shop. He looked awed by the whole affair. "Just waiting for a friend," he told a solicitous clerk.

The clerk looked contemptuously at the old fellow, and turned on his heel. Just then one of his most prized customers rushed past saying, "Dr. Einstein, I hope I did not keep you waiting."

____ Reflection ____

Psychologists today talk a great deal about the images of ourselves we have fashioned. They note that the more confident we become, the freer we are to put aside pretense and act the way we truly wish to.

People who are unconvinced of their own worth and attractiveness are prey to every advertiser's promotion. They will buy shampoo, toothpaste, cologne, designer clothes, name-brand shoes, and almost anything else which promises attractiveness and security. Self-confident people, on the other hand, are not so easily swayed.

Much of what we call sin comes from our own self-doubt and insecurity. Why do we try to impress others by accumulating wealth, power and popularity except that we fear we are not really acceptable without them? Once we understand that we are strong, not because of what we possess but because of what we are, most of life's temptations fall away. The road to sanctity is the road to a proper estimate of our own worth and dignity.

____*Prayer*____

God, my strong and vibrant friend,
>   heal the petty weakness of my heart.
>   Where there is doubt, build confidence.
>   Where there is fear, instill peace.
>   Where there is sullen contempt for others,
>   turn my gaze upon myself
>   that I may discover there
>   the image of your creative joy.

God, my strong and vibrant friend,
>   help me praise your tenderness
>   and touch the world with sympathy
>   born of confidence in the self
>   you created in your finest moment
>   and settled in this awesome world.

God, my strong and vibrant friend,
>   let my heart be strong so that
>   I may enjoy my weakness.

Amen.

Perfection

God: I am weary of people who are intent on being perfect. They try my patience.

Me: But, God, I thought we were supposed to be perfect. The gospel even says, "Be ye perfect the way your heavenly Father is perfect." Perfection is the goal of life, isn't it?

God: It would be fine if people would be perfect in the way I am perfect. The trouble is they have a very different idea of perfection, more like the old scribes and Pharisees.

Me: But, the scribes and Pharisees put Jesus to death. What kind of perfection is that?

God: I know it all sounds confusing to you. That's because you are so far from being perfect, I suppose. Look at it this way. Many religious people are so bent on being good that they begin to believe they can do it on their own, without me. First thing you know, they start looking down their noses at those who don't do things the way they want them done.

Me: Oh, I see. These people are doing the right things for the wrong reasons. They must be the whited sepulchers Jesus mentioned in the gospel. Right?

God: Yes, and they are so tiring. Give me a good, humble sinner any day. It's this piety which covers selfishness and greed I cannot abide. As I said, give me a good, old-fashioned sinner any day.

Me: I guess that means I'm doing all right, God?

God: Yes, you're doing fine. Just don't imagine that you are so perfect that you don't need me.

_____ *A Story* _____

Father Grumblegoose had a dream. In his dream Jesus gave him a special pair of glasses which allowed him to see into the hearts of his parishioners and understand them as God does.

The next morning at Sunday Mass Father Grumblegoose looked through his glasses out across the altar and was stunned to see that some of his finest parishioners had hearts which looked very much like stone. Some teen-agers had hearts turned upside down. Many married people had broken hearts, and some older people had no hearts at all.

Only when Father Grumblegoose looked at the children did he see many hearts filled with what looked like fire. He was terribly confused until he began to read the day's gospel, "Let the little children come unto me. for such is the kingdom of God."

_____ *Reflection* _____

We can easily miss the point as we seek perfection in our spiritual lives. We can become obsessed with obeying all the rules and regulations, saying prayers in the proper order, or fasting on all the right occasions. We may spend so much time on form that we miss the important realities—the poor who are not fed, the old who are forgotten, the children who are abused.

Better for us if we should leave the religious neatness of our lives and go in search of perfection among those in need.

_____ *Prayer* _____

God of all that is untidy, unruly
and unmanageable,
God of sinners passionately striving
to find some hidden love,

God of errant stars and procrastinating
    people,
God of wiggling worms and children
    who do the same,
let your love heal us.
Save us, Lord of all uncertainties,
from hearts that fear the untidy,
from minds that run from uncertainty,
from families that are too proper,
and friends who always know what is right.

Amen.

Family

God: There are very few of my gifts which can compare with family. Creating the family was, I must say, a stroke of genius.

Me: I suppose, God, but my family! We are always arguing, bickering, struggling. Sometimes I think I live in a zoo, not a family.

God: But that's the beauty of it, the arguments, the bickering, the struggling. That's precisely what makes it work so well.

Me: You mean you planned it that way?

God: Not exactly. Remember, I planned the universe in perfect harmony. But once sin entered the world, what better place to learn about life than the family? The family accepts you even at your very worst.

Me: A place to be accepted even when we are our very worst?

God: That's family, and without it what would ever happen to most of you? That, by the way, is what troubles me about these quickie divorces and abandoned children.

Me: I can see that, God. If you divorce without a real struggle to hold the family together, or abandon your children into someone else's keeping, then you have no place to be accepted when you are at your very worst.

God: Now you see what I am driving at. People need to be accepted as they really are, not simply because they behave well. The reason for family bickering, arguing and struggling is love. In a family you struggle with one another; you don't abandon one another. In a family you love much as I do.

_____ *A Story* _____

Once a mother had two sons, both of elementary school age. Never a day went by that the two boys did not argue and fight. They argued over everything from who got into the bathroom first in the morning to who played his radio too loud in the evening.

One day the harried mother called the two boys over to her and said, "From now on I am not going to permit any arguing in this family."

The two boys' faces clouded up and the older boy replied, "Gee, Mom, if we can't argue and fight, we won't have any fun. You're ruining our friendship."

_____ *Reflection* _____

Sigmund Freud tells this parable about the father and sons in a family.

In the beginning the primal herd lived happily under the rule of the primal father. One day a group of the sons decided that they would kill the father and free everyone of his awful rule.

Soon after killing the father and announcing the new freedom to all members of the family, the sons began to notice terrible violence in the primal herd—killing, rape, theft, and more. They feared that the family would disintegrate, so they called everyone together and announced that the spirit of the father had entered into them. To prove this they roasted the flesh of the father and ate it in front of everyone.

Every young adult must kill the father only to later return and claim his spirit. "As my father used to say. . . ."

_____ *Prayer* _____

God, Father of our family,
    heal our rifts and bickering,
    our wars and exploitation,
    our self-seeking and unconcern,
    our greed and anger.

Teach us patience with one another,
     not because our brothers
     and sisters are well-behaved,
     not because everything goes
     the way we want it to,
     not because everyone is gentle
     to our touch,
     but because these are our family —
     black and white,
     rich and poor,
     brown and red and yellow,
     friend and foe,
     all brothers and sisters,
     all children given us to love.
Amen.

Truth

God: What the world needs now is a few good prophets.

Me: Pardon me, God, but we seem to have them. Every night on the news I hear somebody telling the rest of us how to behave. We have every variety of prophet, from far left to far right. If anything, I feel we have too many prophets.

God: You have a point. I can understand how you feel about these voices. It has begun to sound like the old days in Babel. But, what I want is men and women who speak the truth quietly and firmly and are not afraid to face the consequences.

Me: What sort of truth do you have in mind, God?

God: For a start, I would like my prophets to work on honesty.

Me: I remember that from childhood.

God: Yes, and that's about all we ever hear today about honesty—a childhood virtue. I want people to know they must be honest in business, in government, in family life, in shopping, in school, and in every other phase of their lives.

Me: But, God, we have laws to insist on all that.

God: I want people to go beyond the law to basic, grassroots honesty. I would like people to tell the truth, the whole truth, and nothing but the truth.

Me: That takes courage, God, real courage. You would be in trouble all the time. People don't want to hear that kind of truth anymore.

God: But that is the kind of truth I want to hear. No more equivocations, no more advertising "truths," no more public-relations jargon. I would like the truth and people with the courage to speak it.

_____*A Story*_____

Once upon a time God commissioned an angel to slip down to earth and find the glue which held people together. The angel went from town to town and country to country looking for this mysterious glue.

At first she thought the glue must be love, but there were unloving communities that seemed very well stuck together. Then she supposed it was power, but discovered towns that stuck together with very little power.

Just as the angel was about to give up in despair, she saw two people lying to each other. She watched how guarded they were, how braced for deception, how suspicious. Suddenly the angel understood. Speaking the truth, *that* was the glue which held people together. Honesty brought trust and trust was the basis of all human relationships.

_____*Reflection*_____

Erik Erikson, a world famous psychologist, speaks of certain tasks that one must complete in order to mature. The very first task, one which should be accomplished in early infancy, is to learn to trust.

Parents help their children learn this fundamental by being consistently honest, day in and day out, making no exceptions even when it would be much more convenient to do so.

If all human growth rests on our consistent honesty, how easy it is to damage and disillusion children, teen-agers and adults by being less than honest. Each time we behave this way we undermine human growth and do the opposite of what we call evangelization. The basic good news we should learn very early in life is that we can trust someone to tell the truth. Later we may hear the good news of Jesus and, because others have been believable, we can believe him and his unique message.

____*Prayer*____

God,
> you have the courage to speak the truth,
> hard, unpleasant truth at times,
> truth that makes us angry
> so we want to turn away from you.

You never want us so much
> that you make believe,
> coddle us with myths and visions
> that obscure the truth as it really is.

Help us, too, to have that courage
> to speak openly and forthrightly,
> to tell the truth no matter what it costs,
> to speak without blemish,
> to communicate without hiding,
> to share without fearing.

Amen.

Taking Charge

God: Who is in charge of your life?

Me: Why, I am, of course. I am free. I make my own decisions. I am the master of my fate.

God: Unless you turn that responsibility over to someone else. Unless you hire someone else to be your caretaker.

Me: Be my caretaker? I don't understand. How could I, or anyone else for that matter, hire a caretaker to be in charge of my life?

God: People do it every day. Some hire alcohol to be their caretaker. Others try drugs. Still others hand their freedom over to advertisers. I am beginning to think that most of my people don't like being free anymore.

Me: But, God, we treasure freedom. We talk about it all the time. Every year we have hundreds of legal battles over individual freedom. We even enshrined freedom in our constitution. How can you believe that people don't like being free anymore?

God: Look at it from my perspective. I made each person free. I gave each individual a way of life that would bring happiness. Each person was to make his or her own decisions, to be in charge of the life I gave. It is not working out that way. Too often, people behave like sheep. There is so little individuality, so little taking charge of one's own life.

Me: I see, God, but I never thought of it that way. You want all of us to be distinct and different, to march to our own drummers, so to speak.

God: Right. I want each person to be in charge of his or her own life. And don't forget, I'm always around to help you.

_____ *A Story* _____

In the fourth century, all Roman males were expected to serve in the army, especially if their fathers had done so before them. Everyone followed the custom and, since battles were few, most men returned home loaded with honors and without many scars.

Maximilian was called to serve. After thought and prayer he refused to enlist, even though his own father had been a decorated military leader and Christians of Maximilian's time saw no evil in military service.

"I respect others' decisions to serve," said young Maximilian, "but my conscience tells me clearly that I cannot serve in the army. I cannot and will not kill another human being no matter how noble the cause."

For his refusal to enlist, young Maximilian was beheaded. He had taken charge of his life.

_____ *Reflection* _____

The less secure people are, the more they follow the crowd. But when people come to understand their own unique personalities more completely and to glory in them, they break away from the crowd and do things because they believe they are right.

As some individuals become fully rooted in their own personalities, they will even return to the group and try to influence the way it behaves. First, they move away from the group and then return to it in order to give it direction.

This moving away into solitude followed by a return is captured in the motto of the medieval saint, Dominic, who said, "contemplate first and then share with others." Without the withdrawal, the solitude, the contemplation, without first taking charge, we have little to share.

____*Prayer*____

God, you who are alone but not lonely,
    cure my fear of solitude.
Teach me the beauty of life's deserts,
    the music of the tunes I alone can hear,
    the drum beats that are my own rhythm,
    the notes that are sung for me alone.

God, you who are not afraid of people,
    cure my fear of multitudes.
Teach me the goodness of the crowd,
    the warmth and wonder of my own kind,
    the joy of being with another,
    the excitement that only friendship brings.

God, you who are One and Three,
    let me be distinct from every other,
    a life lived in splendid isolation,
    yet entwined with other lives
    which, like mine, pulse to rhythms
    which only you and they can hear.

Amen.

Discipline

God: I have been thinking about discipline today.

Me: Please, God, speak quietly. We are having such a hard time getting people to believe in you as it is. If you start talking about something as old fashioned as discipline, you will set our work back 20 years.

God: But I believe in discipline.

Me: Can't you call it something else, God, something like "creative correction," "personality persuasion," or "socially interactive direction"? Anything, God, but discipline. Believe me, it just won't sell.

God: Why?

Me: Discipline is a harsh word and nobody today wants to be thought of as harsh.

God: But I discipline and certainly I am not harsh. Discipline springs from love and you cannot love unless you discipline. Are you saying that people today don't love enough to discipline?

Me: I don't know, God. We like to think of ourselves as friends and counselors, not as disciplinarians, not as people who force others to do what we want done.

God: That means that you are afraid, doesn't it? You fear the responsibility of directing another toward me? Why are you afraid?

Me: We might be wrong. We might make a mistake. We might damage a child's psyche, for example.

God: You can do no greater damage to a child and make no more awesome mistake than to fail to give firm direction, to discipline.

Me: We really do have to be disciplinarians, then?

God: You do. Love for your children and your friends demands it. Without discipline, there can be no true love, only pretense.

____A Story____

An experienced teacher once said to a young colleague, "All young people must cut their teeth on someone. You do them, their families, and the whole community a distinct favor if you let them cut their teeth on you."

This advice gave Bill the courage to fight with Carl, a 10th-grade student who never did his homework properly. After school they sat in the classroom hour after hour—Carl occasionally cursing under his breath when he thought Bill could not hear. It was a battle of the wills and, in the end, Bill won.

Every year on Bill's birthday Carl, who is a teacher himself now, calls to say happy birthday—even though he left the class 30 years ago!

____Reflection____

One American psychologist says that all of us have a "looking-glass self." We do not see ourselves directly; instead, we rely on what others seem to see when they look at us. Our impression of self is gleaned from the thousands of mirrors other people hold up to us in everyday life.

If this is true, and to a degree it surely is, then how important unanimity is among parents, teachers, church leaders, and other significant people in a young person's life. The more consistent the reflections, the clearer the youngster's image becomes.

If all of us react firmly and consistently to the behavior of a child, if we all reward the same things and punish the same things, then most of the work of discipline is done.

___Prayer___

Lord, I thank you for the discipline
    that is built into my life.
Fire pains my hand to warn me that
    it is already burning at my flesh.
My feet ache to warn me that
    nails have grown into tender flesh.
My dog barks unmercifully to remind me that
    I have forgotten it is time to feed.
People snarl at me to say that
    my snarling will not be tolerated.
Children sit frozen and unloving to say
    that my anger is uncalled for.
All around me animals, things and people
    discipline my unruly ego.
Thank you, God, for life's disciplining.
Without it, what would become of me?
Amen.

Mercy

God: Every Sunday you repeat "Lord, have mercy" and "Lamb of God, have mercy on us."

Me: Every Sunday, God. I'm right up front where you can see me.

God: Good. But what does this word *mercy* mean to you?

Me: Ah, that's easy. It means "forgive me for I have sinned." Mercy is the sort of thing a powerful person gives to one of his servants, right?

God: Wrong. Mercy means much more than that. It means that I love you so intensely that my love heals you. When you say "Lord, have mercy," you are saying "Lord, love me so intensely that I am healed."

Me: Wow, I never knew that.

God: Yes, that's what the old Hebrew word meant, but as time passed much of the word's fire got lost. I would like to know what it really means so you can pray that way.

Me: Does it also mean that I must love other people so intensely that I heal them as well?

God: Of course. Husbands are supposed to heal their wives, wives their husbands, parents their children, children their parents. Love can heal the worst pain.

Me: That certainly gives me a new vision of marriage and family life. I had always thought of it as a contract. You know what I mean—rights, obligations and all that sort of thing.

God: Oh, that's all right, but it doesn't begin to go far enough. I want husbands and wives to be like my son, Jesus, and the church, so loving and so loved that people are healed at the deepest level. That's what he meant when he told his listeners that I desire mercy, not sacrifice.

____A Story____

Hannah was a cruel little girl. At seven, she seemed to enjoy striking other children, kicking adults, screaming out her contempt for anyone who came near her, and spending long hours sitting all alone in a darkened room.

The doctors who were treating Hannah in the hospital knew that both her parents had died in an automobile accident, and that Hannah had never adjusted to a foster home. They had tried every known medical approach and were considering sending Hannah to an institution.

Then, without warning, the little girl began to smile, to relax, and to be less aggressive. The doctors were amazed. What had happened?

After a long investigation the doctors discovered that an old hospital cleaning lady was visiting Hannah and staying after working hours with her. The old woman said very little. She just held Hannah's tiny hand and sang softly to her.

What modern medicine could not heal, an old woman's love could and did.

____Reflection____

Alcoholics Anonymous was the first of more than a dozen groups that help people come to grips with their problems. There are similar programs to help with obesity, bad tempers, permissiveness, drug abuse and more.

All these groups follow a similar format. The person seeking healing must first admit that he or she has a problem. Once that problem is out in the open, a schedule of life is organized. Finally, a support group helps the individual meet the demand of this new schedule.

These groups know that change is difficult. We need friends to support and encourage us. A loving community has the power to heal.

____Prayer____

Lord, God of tender mercy,
>   love and heal our dispirited world—
>   men who feel alien and alone,
>   women who substitute domination for love,
>   children who cannot live in their parents' house,
>   infants deprived of tenderness and compassion.

Lord, God of tender mercy,
>   love and heal our uncertain church—
>   priests who feel unappreciated and discouraged,
>   men who can sacrifice but do not know mercy,
>   women who feel deprived and degraded,
>   children who feel they are not welcome.

Lord, God of tender mercy,
>   love and heal me.

My wounds and scars are many—
>   some long forgotten, some brand-new,
>   some inflicted by my parents
>   and some visited on me in later years.

Love me so intensely that
>   I am healed of every wound.

Amen.

Trust

God: I would like you to become like a little child. My son, Jesus, told you that.

_Me:_ I know, I know. But, God, do you realize how difficult that is today with all our education and experience? The gulf between adults and children is wider than it ever was before.

God: Sadly, I know. The trip back to childhood is longer and longer, harder and harder, but it must be made. You do understand that?

_Me:_ Not really, God. There must be some other way. I love little children, but how can I ever become like one? And why do you insist on such a strange thing, something so out of keeping with our modern world?

God: Why do you love little children?

_Me:_ Well, I guess because they look up to me; they think I will help them. Little children trust me when nobody else does.

God: Ah. Is it so strange that I should like all my children to react to me in the same way, to look up to me, to know I will help them, to trust them?

_Me:_ But, God, children have to act that way. They are helpless, and unless we adults reach out to them they won't make it.

God: And you are different?

_Me:_ Well, no, I suppose not when I really think about it. It is just that I hate to admit it. I like to play at being independent and pretend that I am powerful enough to go it alone.

God: Now, who's being childish?

Me: I am.

God: Since you are going to be either childish or childlike, one or the other, why not admit the truth and become like a little child in your relationship with me? Once you find the trust of a child, you will find happiness.

_____ A Story _____

Kim and Don were engaged to be married when Kim saw Don at lunch with a beautiful young woman. Her heart was broken. How could she marry such a faithless man?

After she calmed down a bit, Kim thought to herself, "Everything I know about Don runs counter to what I saw this afternoon. Even though I saw him with my own eyes, my mind and heart tell me there must be something here I do not understand." Though shaken, Kim continued to trust.

That evening Don talked with Kim about his day and casually mentioned that he had had lunch with his aunt, a woman not much older than he.

Kim's struggle had been to trust her heart in spite of appearances, as a child does. Isn't that our challenge too?

_____ Reflection _____

An infant's first emotional response is not love but trust. Infants must trust that others will not hurt them, drop them, or fail to feed, change and cuddle them. They must rely totally upon others.

In our relationship with God, we must continue to be the trusting infant. We continue to rely on him for each breath we take, the food we eat, everything we need. To acknowledge this truth is to be trusting, truthful and humble. To deny it is to be skeptical, deceitful and proud. The first three characteristics we call childlike, the last three childish. The child is, one way or the other, always within us.

___Prayer___

Lord, Father of all life,
    how difficult it is to admit
    I need you for my every breath,
    my daily bread,
    mercy and forgiveness, too.
I would rather be my own person,
    independent, powerful, alone.
Yet the truth keeps popping up
    no matter how I try to hide it.
It is in every illness that afflicts me,
    in every love gone sour,
    in every failure in my life,
    in every opportunity forever lost.
Humbly I come to ask for daily bread
    and know my need for so much more —
    for life, for friends, for love.
Because I ask, you know I trust,
    if not every day
    at least on the days
    the sun will not shine.
Amen.

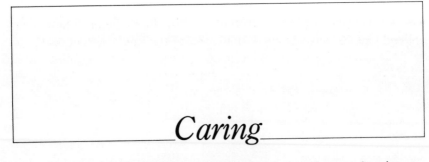

Caring

God: Have you noticed how psychological jargon keeps showing up in the media? It's a problem.

Me: You don't mean to condemn psychology, do you?

God: No, no, not at all. It's this pop psychology, quack psychology, that can be dangerous for so many of my children. They sometimes believe the most absurd things.

Me: Are there any good psychologists?

God: Oh, yes. Remember Sigmund Freud? He was especially helpful in discovering that the direction of a person's life will focus either outward, toward others, or inward, toward self. Of course, theologians had been teaching that for centuries. Still, it was insightful.

Me: I suppose that this direction outward is what we call caring?

God: Precisely. When you reach out to others, you care for them. When you think only of self, you care only about yourself. One way leads to happiness in this life and the next; the other leads to cynicism and bitterness here and hereafter. Freud was right, you see. Psychology can and often is a real help, but watch out for the jargon.

_____*A Story*_____

One day a very famous author died and went up to the pearly gates. He had written over 100 books about God and religion and thought it well to bring all of them with him to show Saint Peter. The writer noticed that he was not alone, for many in the line also had books.

He asked the woman in front of him if she was an author too. "No," she smiled back, "all I ever did was take care of children, first my own, then a sister's, then my daughter's. My whole life was children, children, children. I have nothing to show for it."

"But, those books in your hand?"

"Oh, those are the lists of people I cared about. I understand that you have to have them to get into heaven. I see you have lots of books. You must have cared about many people."

Suddenly the author realized that he had brought the wrong books.

____ *Reflection* ____

There is a myth that once we begin to care about others, others will care about us. The truth is that there will be many different responses to our caring, some negative and some positive.

Some will resent our caring and see in it a challenge to their own apathy. Others will imagine that our caring for other people somehow diminishes our love for them. Still others will think our caring meddlesome. And, there will always be those who believe our caring is a sign that we are guilt-ridden or neurotic.

Yes, some will eventually see in our caring a sign for rejoicing, but usually those people are quiet for a long, long time until they are sure we are acting from a pure motive.

Caring brings joy only when we do it because it is right and is its own reward. If we look to others for affirmation and appreciation, we may be sorely disappointed and even give up.

____ *Prayer* ____

God, you care
  for the tiny dewdrop's perfect roundness,
  for the rock's layers of unmixed color,
  for the forest's varied hues of green,

for the baby's plaintive cry,
for the child's brightening smile,
for the adolescent's uncertain tread,
for the parents' bouncy happiness
    that their child is born,
for the older woman's grief
    that the friend of years is gone.
God, you are compassionate.
You enter into our own passions,
    joyful and sad,
    and live them through with us.
God, caring and compassionate,
    be ever at my side, be my guide.

Amen.

Money

God: Do you think most Americans trust in God?

Me: Well, I really don't know, God. Isn't that a strange question for you of all people to ask?

God: Have you ever noticed that all your coins and bills carry the words, "In God we trust"?

Me: I did know that, but I must say I don't remember ever looking for the words.

God: I was wondering if we couldn't add a few more words to that little motto to make it a bit more accurate.

Me: What would you add, God?

God: ". . . When all else fails." That might be a bit more accurate, don't you think? "In God we trust when all else fails."

Me: You are probably right, God. As long as there is plenty of money and plenty to buy, we don't think too much about you. But if our money fails, or if we lose our power to purchase, then we come running right back to you.

God: The love of money is the root of all evil.

Me: True, God. I know you are right—war, slavery, discrimination, injustice, abuse and all other evils have their root in a desire for money and the power money brings.

God: Why, then, is my name on your money? It is an affront. Why

not put my name on your plans to care for the poor, your pro-
posals for peace, your foreign aid and food for peace programs?
Why on money? My son, Jesus, said that no one can serve me
and money at the same time. This is still true, even in these
most modern times.

____ *A Story* ____

George Eliot, the British novelist, told the tale of Silas Marner, a
greedy, withdrawn miser of a man. He exploited and manipulated,
hated and was hated. His whole life was dominated by a desire to
acquire and own.

When Silas was at the height of his power, a little orphan girl
entered his life. Her love destroyed Silas's greed. As his greed died,
so too did his withdrawal from the village, his hatred and exploitation
of others. People came to understand and love the former miser, and
he took his place happily in the community.

____ *Reflection* ____

Economics, the study of wealth, is often called the dismal science. Its
conclusions always have about them a harsh edge and seem to forebode
disaster to one group or another.

As long as our happiness is pegged to the marketplace, we can
expect that sometimes, at least, we will be unhappy. No nation enjoys
prosperity all the time.

The love of money leads to desperate acts when the economy
falls upon evil days. After the famous crash of 1929 some financiers
committed suicide, others murder, still others left families and went
into hiding. Today's money crunch is leading many to desperate deeds:
theft, arson, exploitation and fraud.

In times of economic growth, believing that we do not care that
much for money is relatively easy. When depression threatens, however, we discover just how much we depend on money and the things
and power money buys.

____*Prayer*____

Lord, creator of all that is,
>I want to love all of your creation,
>and not retreat into a world
>which holds some creation good and some bad.

I want to be able to love both men and women,
>the young and the old,
>the poor and the rich,
>the peacemakers and those who wage war.

Help me to see the good in all creation,
>but to keep first things first—
>people before power over them,
>love before greed's tortured way,
>friendship before ownership of things or people,
>tender compassion before cruel domination.

Amen.

Bravery

God: I want to talk to you about an outmoded word, one nobody mentions any longer.

Me: What is the word, God?

God: Bravery.

Me: You're right, God. It is outmoded. It brings to mind "Onward Christian Soldiers," and the slap on the cheek at confirmation. Definitely old hat. Glad you don't intend to use it, God.

God: But I do intend to use it. I see more and more cowardice in this modern world, and I want to issue a call to bravery among my people.

Me: Frankly, God, bravery has a military ring and the military is out. We are into peace today.

God: I am in favor of peace, certainly, but that takes bravery. One must be quite brave to stand up and espouse peace when so many people make their living building weapons of war.

Me: But, God, bravery smacks of militarism and imperialism.

God: Nonsense. The reason bravery doesn't sit very well today is that so many people are not brave at all. They have adopted bureau-speak as a language and manage to sound as though they agree with all sides of a question. They are not brave enough to confront others and say exactly what they believe.

Me: Don't you think that's a bit strong, God, begging your pardon?

God: Perhaps, but it is true. Too many of my people sound soft and convictionless. I'd like to breathe a little of the old time prophet into them. Let them call evil, evil and sin, sin. Let them be brave enough to stand for or against something.

___A Story___

Ronaldo was 16 when local drug pushers first tried to interest him in their wares. They appealed to his manliness by laughing at sissies who refused drugs. When this did not work, they introduced him to the girl of his dreams. She insisted that their love be made perfect with drugs. Again, Ronaldo refused.

Ronaldo knew who the pushers were, but was afraid to report them. Perhaps the police themselves were part of the drug ring. His conscience continued to prod him. Finally, very secretly, he informed on the pushers. A week later Ronaldo's mutilated body was found in a trash bag in an alley.

Call him foolish or call him brave, Ronaldo died for what he believed was right, a city free from the corrupting influence of drug peddlers.

___Reflection___

The devil is said to be the father of lies but we must wonder if a desire to be popular is not their mother. Many insecure people want to please everyone. Pleasing everyone comes at a price, and that price is usually the truth.

Our society does not reward or lionize the brave people who alienate others rather than betray their convictions. Outspokenness is not a popular virtue. We prefer to use the clever word or the hidden innuendo to make a point. Such speech seems more civil to us because it is not confrontational.

Our idea of Christianity is often devoid of controversy and strong words. Jesus is made to appear so gentle that he seems afraid to speak strongly to anyone. Yet the gospels reveal Jesus as a very brave young man, one who did not hesitate to confront the powers of his own day.

_____*Prayer*_____

God, forthright and determined,
    you who sent the prophets and their message,
    you who demanded justice before piety,
    you who stood before the Sanhedrin unashamed,
    you who drove buyers and sellers from the Temple,
    you who called your woe upon the rich
    and called hardhearted adults to become like children,
hear these frightened prayers of ours.

Wipe away our fears of other people
    and the evil they can do to us,
    their sharp tongues,
    their strong words,
    their derisive glances.
Give us the bravery to stand and be counted
    for what is right and true and good
    no matter what the cost to us.

Amen.

Sex

God: I imagine many people will read this page before they read many of the others. Why do you Americans have such an adolescent preoccupation with sex?

Me: Adolescent, God? Why do you say we are adolescent?

God: Adolescents, who are new to sexuality, love to talk about it, can't get it off their minds, think that nothing in life matters more. Now, that's fine for adolescents but you should outgrow some of that.

Me: Outgrow? God, what do you mean? Outgrow sex?

God: Oh, that's not what I said at all. What I said was you should outgrow this compulsion to talk about it all the time, to make snide remarks and to focus your whole attention on it.

Me: What takes the place of sex?

God: Love does. Don't you see? Sex in the context of love, true lasting love, means something quite different from sex for sex's sake. Sex's meaning comes from its surroundings. It can be an act of hatred and violence as in rape, an act of selfishness and self-concern as in casual sex, or it can be something beautiful and deeply moving as in real love.

Me: Yes, God, I do understand. You meant it to be beautiful, didn't you?

God: I did. That's why marriage is the best place for it. Even in marriage, love takes time to grow. But, the stability is there and the commitment to a future. Sex is safer in such an environment.

Me: If only you had designed us a little differently so that we wanted only what is good! Couldn't you have done it that way?

God: Not and leave you truly free. That was my dilemma. I had to have creatures who never made mistakes or free creatures who did all sorts of silly things. You know which choice I made.

_____ *A Story* _____

According to legend, a young man who wished to leave his family was locked in a castle room. Late one night, as the young man lay sleeping, the door opened and a beautiful young woman entered. She lay down beside the man and began to touch him gently.

He awoke in a few moments to discover his body on fire with desire for the sensuous woman. He strode to the opposite end of the room, grabbed up a burning brand from the fireplace, and drove the woman out.

Impressed by his resolve the young man's evil brothers allowed him to leave the family castle and go out to do the work of the Lord.

Variations of this legend are told about several medieval saints including Thomas Aquinas. Beneath the story lurks the belief that we must come to grips with our own personality before we can do much for the kingdom of the Lord.

_____ *Reflection* _____

Sex sells almost everything from automobiles to detergents, from records to books, from clothing to housing. Advertisers learned long ago that the way to people's pocketbooks is through their fantasies. If people imagine that a product will make them more attractive and lovable, they will buy it.

We do want to be lovable, and like our ancient forebears, we are still looking for some magic way to become what we desire to be. The truth is we can be both attractive and lovable only by becoming less selfish and more generous.

____ *Prayer* ____

Is there sex in heaven, Lord?
Or at least some deep abiding love
    so that I will not be alone up there,
    unfit and feeling I do not belong?
Is there sex in heaven, Lord?
Or at least some deep intertwining
    of some human spirits so that I
    will be with another who knows and understands
    and cares about the real me?
Is there sex in heaven, Lord?
Or at least some companionship,
    not limited as friendships are now,
    able to leap within my heart and heal its hurts,
    love so powerful that it makes me free?
No, Lord, I know there is no sex in heaven,
    perhaps because there is no need for it.
There we will know as we are known
    and dark mirrors will be put aside.
We shall be so happy we will not even wonder,
    Is there sex in heaven?
Amen.

Kindness

God: Why is it that everybody believes in kindness, but so few practice it?

Me: Is that a real question, God, or merely a rhetorical groan?

God: Probably a bit of both. Why are people, corporations, and even nations so unkind?

Me: I think we would like to be kind, God, but the price is too high. I want to be kind to the postman, for example, but I know that if I am tomorrow's mail will be in someone else's box. Let down a minute and people take advantage every time.

God: You make the world sound like a jungle.

Me: It is, God. It's dog-eat-dog out there. It may not look that way from where you sit, but closeup it's "every man for himself."

God: With an attitude like that I can understand why there is so little kindness.

Me: Try it, God, and you will see.

God: I did try it. They persecuted and crucified my son, Jesus. You are partially right, but what is your defensiveness doing to you? Are you becoming cynical, bitter, hostile and alienated?

Me: I suppose I am, God, but it takes a hard shell to survive.

God: Perhaps, then, survival isn't worth the price. Have you forgotten about turning the other cheek? about doing good to those who harm you? about the nobility of suffering persecution for what is right? If you are going to be a Christian, you must take the punches that come with being kind. You do want to be a Christian, don't you?

____*A Story*____

A young mother discovered a magic bottle one day while digging in her backyard. As she cleaned the bottle, a voice came out of the container, "Ask for one favor and it will be granted to you."

Quickly the women replied, "May I always be kind."

"Granted," said the voice.

That morning the young mother spanked her children, confronted her mother-in-law about her meddling, spoke to the butcher about the tainted meat she had bought the week before. During the afternoon she cut off a neighbor who wanted to gossip about a mutual friend and cooked her husband's favorite meal.

____*Reflection*____

Kindness is *not* acting in a saccharine manner to other people. True Christian kindness grows out of a solid respect for ourselves, for others, and for God.

Once we read and accept the opening chapters of Genesis, something profound happens. If all people are made to the image and likeness of God, then every human being demands the same respect one affords God.

About the only way to get around repecting others is to deny that God himself is worthy of respect. The stories of communism and Nazi Germany are such tales. To treat millions of human beings like cattle, or worse, leaders of these movements had to deny that God has meaning.

In our society the existence of God and belief in him play an important part in moderating greed and selfishness and enabling us to practice true kindness. While individuals and groups may from time to time be blind to the implications of God's existence in everyday life, that meaning will assert itself again and again and, with urgency, turn society upside down.

____Prayer____

God of tenderness and compassion,
    kind and loving Father of the poor and powerless,
    strengthen our backbones
    that we may be meek but never weak,
    peacemakers but never at the price of justice,
    mourners but never embroiled in self-pity,
    poor in spirit but never shiftless and unconcerned,
    merciful but always ready to confront,
    ready to suffer persecution but strong in our defense
        of others' rights,
    pure in heart but never fanatic in our search for right.
God of tenderness and compassion,
    kind and loving Father of the poor and powerless,
    strengthen our backbones
    that we may not flee confrontation,
    never flinch in a fight for what is right,
    never turn away from another's pain,
    always champion the cause of right,
    be endlessly with you to complain
    together about evil in the world,
    show respect for everyone,
    and never turn from kindness in the battle.

Amen.

Reverence

God: Do you ever talk about reverence anymore?

Me: No, God, that's a word from the past. You will have to admit that a lot of what passed for reverence was really hypocrisy.

God: True, but it was helpful to many of my children, especially the younger ones. It is the only way young children learn that I am someone special.

Me: Well, all right, if it's for children.

God: Of course there are always some adults who need a bit of reverence, too. Those who don't have much of a religious life during the week need marks of reverence to help them change gears and focus on holy things on Sunday.

Me: Well, I suppose so, God, children and adults without much religious background.

God: Oh, there's one more group.

Me: Who is that, God?

God: The people who are around the church all the time—priests, sisters, active lay people. Without reverence, they have a way of forgetting why they are there. Church becomes just another building.

Me: Yes, you're right, God. We do need that. Wait a minute! If we add children, adults without much day-to-day religion and those active in the parish, we have everyone.

God: It would seem so. Everyone needs a sense of reverence. It doesn't have to be the old form of reverence you used as a child, but all human beings need ways of reminding themselves, if no one else, that they are doing something special at church. Times of silence, deliberate bows, careful genuflections, prayers said with fervor all help capture the spirit of reverence everyone needs.

____ A Story ____

One very old bishop who lived many years ago had a remarkable habit. In those days people genuflected to kiss the bishop's ring. He allowed it as did all bishops of the day. As soon as the genuflector was on his feet, however, this bishop dropped to his knees and asked for the person's blessing.

The old bishop believed in reverence and remembered that all his people were God's own children and carried within them his Holy Spirit.

____ Reflection ____

Reverence is no more than an outward sign of an inner respect one person bears for another. There was a time when men tipped their hats to ladies, not to all women but to ladies. There was a time when people of all ages bowed before the priest carrying the blessed sacrament. There was a time when people did not call one another by given names until they knew each other well.

The problem with reverence is that the outward signs can exist without the inward respect. In these cases the reverence is no more than sham and hypocrisy. Yet small acts of reverence for another person do have a way of recalling to us the wonder and awe of another person.

Our contemporary culture is low on marks of reverence. This may be one reason we have so little respect for other human beings. We may be suspicious of reverences for officials and the powerful, but why not accord the poor and powerless some marks of deep respect and reverence? They are, after all, the very special friends of God.

____*Prayer*____

God, creator of this world of ours
    and all the far-flung stars
    and of the world beyond the stars,
I bow my head before you.
Slowly and with care my head is bowed.
This bow says to me
    and to you, O Lord,
        that you are great and good.

God, creator of this world of ours,
    and all its many peoples rich and poor
    and of every race's little ones,
I bow my head before all.
Slowly and with care my head is bowed.
This bow says to me
    and to you, O Lord,
        that they, too, are great and good.

Amen.

Futuring

God: I notice that there are several new magazines about futuring and even a society for futurists. What do you think about the future?

Me: I am confused, God. I hear about the electronic marvels: computers, television breakthroughs, new crop strains, sources for energy that will not pollute, laser beams that will make war impossible and, I dare to hope, lead to a better world.

God: Yes, but . . .

Me: I know how selfish and evil we humans can be and I have to wonder whether we will not use these new inventions as stupidly as we have already used the printing press, the automobile, the airplane, the atomic bomb, and all the rest.

God: Pulled in two directions?

Me: Yes, God. And the churches are the same way. Some churches preach doom and destruction all the time. Others talk of our unlimited future and how you will soon be with us because we are doing so well. I'm not sure that my good sense lets me believe either view.

God: Three cheers for your good sense.

Me: What do you mean, God?

God: You are right that the future will not be all doom and destruction. There has always been someone on the street corner promising the end of the world. And there have always been false prophets telling people what they wanted to hear. Life here on earth will always be a mixture of joy and sorrow, challenge and catastrophy. With all that said, it is and was and will be beautiful.

_____A Story_____

The ancient Greeks had an interest in futuring. They told the story of Cassandra, a woman who had displeased the gods. As a punishment she was given the ability to see the future, but warned that no one would ever believe her predictions.

Cassandra did warn her countrymen of every coming catastrophe only to be dismissed angrily. In fact, so many thought her mad that she became a kind of patron of the insane.

You know there is more in this old myth than meets the eye — especially if you have ever had a glimpse into the future and tried to convince others of your insight.

_____Reflection_____

As we approach the year 2,000 we can expect many predictions of the end of time. History tells us that a kind of madness seized Europe just before the end of the first millennia.

Some members of our human community are always ready for the end to come. They seem to lust after some cataclysm that will end the dreary lives they lead. They reason that the end of all things is better than the day-to-day struggles to bring the kingdom into the nooks and crannies of human life.

Yet we must continue to ponder the parable of the mustard seed. According to the parable the kingdom of God grows very slowly, branch by branch, leaf by leaf.

Or, we should turn to the parable of the yeast and imagine ourselves tiny bits of yeast punching diligently against the mass of dough and never seeing it rise.

To understand the power of the kingdom we must stand back and view history in large bits, three hundred to four hundred years, and then assess its growth. Meanwhile, like the yeast and the mustard seed, it's one day at a time.

_____ *Prayer* _____

Lord of light and understanding,
 what shall my future be?
Shall I grow like the tiny mustard seed
 into a life of strength and purpose?
Shall I, instead, be like the dutiful yeast
 and spend my years helping others to rise
 and never see the value of my efforts?
Shall I . . . shall I?
Why do I ask, O Lord, for do you not speak?
You have told me once that my future will be glorious —
 for eye has not seen,
 nor ear heard,
 nor has it entered into the mind of man,
 the glory you have prepared for those who love you.
That must be enough.
And it is, Lord.
Amen.

Mary

God: I have noticed that you don't talk with Mary anymore. How come?

Me: Well, God, now that I feel so much at ease with you I don't bother going through an intermediary.

God: Are you saying that she isn't very useful to you anymore?

Me: That's an awful way to put it, God.

God: But is it true?

Me: Well, perhaps it is. I don't like to think that I am so self-centered that I used her to get to you, and now that I feel so relaxed with you I have tossed her aside.

God: But, it does seem that way, doesn't it? You are the loser, by the way.

Me: How am I the loser, God?

God: Right now you are struggling to understand the roles of men and women. You are bent on finding an equality that does not do violence to family life. And here is Mary, a most independent woman with a penchant for the family.

Me: Do you mean that Mary could well be the model we are looking for?

God: Could be, if you will strip away what centuries of artists, poets and theologians have done to her.

Me: You mean go back to the New Testament?

God: Exactly. You will find a woman with an independent spirit, answerable only to me, unafraid of what people said, willing to challenge her son, loyal in spite of a threat of death, full of courage. Mary had a sensitivity, too, a winsomeness and gentility which can be a model for men as well as women.

Yes, you are missing a lot when you forget Mary. She is an extraordinary person and a remarkable woman.

____ A Story ____

There is a fabled town in India where men are routinely considered servants and women the ruling class. Centuries ago all noble men were killed in battle and the noble women, forced by necessity, married slaves. From that day to this women make all decisions, control all wealth and lead their town while the men do household chores and remain behind closed doors.

The town is not known for its peacefulness nor for its gentility. It is no more just than the towns around it. Nor is it any worse.

A wise visitor to the town remarked, "Power makes souls brittle in women as in men. Only the poor in spirit ever manage to discover life's full joy."

____ Reflection ____

In the days of chivalry men were taught an elaborate etiquette toward women who were, in fact, powerless. Chivalry protected the women against the worst barbarisms of aggressive men.

In these days when ideally woman's talents bring as much honor and power as a man's, perhaps we need a new kind of chivalry. We need a chivalry not to protect women, but to protect men and women who are powerless from those who are aggressively powerful. What about a chivalry toward the old, the poor, the uneducated, the sick? Mary identifies with these powerless people. If we recapture a respect and love for her, we might begin to think more of her brothers and sisters who are insignificant and small.

_____ *Prayer* _____

Mary, mother of the Lord,
    have we forgotten you?
Have we become so strident
    and full of our own importance
    that your village life seems dull
    and uninspiring?
Mary, mother of the Lord,
    have our lives become
    so centered on power and prestige
    that we have forgotten it is people
    and being bound to them
    that makes us free?
Mary, mother of the Lord,
    look on your uncertain children,
    strident, aggressive, fearful of our lives,
    and send us peace and order
    and a new respect for all of God's children
    whoever they may be.
Amen.

Love

God: Do you think most of my children know that I am love.

Me: You know better than I, God. But if it were left up to me to judge, I'd say most people never think of you that way. They think of your power, your strength, your wisdom perhaps, but love? No, I don't think they are comfortable thinking of you as love.

God: You're right, sad to say. Most people are embarrassed by a God who is love. They may acknowledge that in some abstract way, but it is so much easier to say, "God will punish you," than to say, "God loves you."

Me: Yes, God, we are embarrassed. I think that's really it. We don't like to think that the whole creative process is in the hands of someone soft. We prefer a hard and just manager, one who deals out justice and does it strictly.

God: Love *is* justice.

Me: How can love be justice? Justice means handing out punishments, totalling up accounts, checking to see that we get what's coming to us. Love is something else, isn't it?

God: Love is wanting what is best for everyone.

Me: How does that fit in with justice?

God: Easily enough. Those punishments you see are medicine to help my children grow, loving medicine. All that accounting is your idea of justice, not mine. If I see the slightest hope in a human personality, I bend to nurture it. Sin is its own punishment. My task is to love the hell out of my children.

Me: That's a funny way to put it, God.

God: But it's true. I do not love because you are already good. No, I love you so that you can become good. All that is necessary is that you recognize this good news and respond to it. My love will do the rest.

_____A Story_____

Once a monk lived in the desert, ate only bread and water, and spent years in prayer. His skin was burned from the desert air, his stomach flattened by his fasting, and his knees calloused from kneeling in incessant prayer. On day the monk died, fully expecting that he would have a very high place in heaven.

When he arrived in heaven and was assigned a place very far from God, he began to be dispirited and angry. Above him were men and women who had never entered the desert, never fasted, and prayed very little. "This place is not fair," the monk thought to himself.

Saint Peter heard his grumbling and said, "Now, if you want justice, we do have a place where justice is accurately measured."

"Fine," smiled the old monk. "Give me justice any day."

Off he went to hell.

_____Reflection_____

We have hundreds of stories of parents who love the most outrageous children. Convicted murderers can often claim the company of their mothers and fathers during the days before their execution. Women who have disgraced their families find it easy to return to an aging mother and father and be welcomed with complete joy.

Experiences like these made the story of the prodigal son credible to the people of Jesus' day. Everyone understood that a good father would welcome his errant son back, no matter how wickedly he had behaved. Life was like that.

Why, then, should we expect less of God? Why do we try to bind God to our narrow little ideas of justice when so many human parents go far beyond them? Is God less loving than parents are?

____Prayer____

God, loving and compassionate,
   do not treat me justly,
   no eye for an eye or tooth for a tooth,
   no strict measurement of my growth,
   no accounting or audit of my good and evil.
Instead, treat me as your errant child.
Forgive my faults,
   love me into virtue,
   tempt me into love,
   be patient with my evils
   until they fall away
   and are forgotten.
Reconcile me to you, to others,
   and to my better self.
Save me, not because I am good,
   but because you are.

Amen.

Jubilee

God: Have you ever heard of the ancient Hebrew jubilee?

Me: No, God, I don't think I have.

God: Every 50 years all debts were forgiven, slaves were freed, land was given back to its original owners, and all fields were allowed to lie fallow. Israelites rested and prayed for a year.

Me: Astounding, God. Did they actually do that?

God: Never perfectly, but it was their ideal.

Me: That would certainly play havoc with our modern, industrial societies. It takes initiative to get things going, and maybe a little greed to acquire and maintain the capital necessary for business.

God: I know, and it is this greed which troubles me.

Me: But, God, you don't want to kill personal initiative and have everyone depend on the government for everything, do you?

God: No, but people must always come before things. I want to see *all* my children fed, housed, educated, given medical care, and enjoying a measure of political and religious freedom.

Me: God, you're an idealist! We have to have unemployment to control inflation, capital to produce jobs, war to weed out the weak. These are all necessary evils in the world, aren't they?

God: I never planned it that way. Only sin has made such things seem necessary. I judge a nation not by what it owns, but by how it distributes what it has to its own members and to those in need throughout the world. Maybe your country could use a jubilee.

_____ *A Story* _____

Once upon a time there was a strange power surge, and the computer which controlled all credit information for a huge company erased all its records. The president of the company appeared on television and announced that all debts were cancelled. Rather than try to investigate millions of accounts, the company had decided to begin all over again. Millions of people were suddenly without debt. It was a modern jubilee.

Some people were overjoyed. Others were angry because they had already paid part of their credit card debt and felt that this was not fair. They said that the company's action encouraged laziness and should be condemned.

On observer remarked, "This sounds like the parable of the laborers in the vineyard." No one bothered to argue.

_____ *Reflection* _____

Pope John XXIII wrote a masterful encyclical called *Peace On Earth*. Scholars from every part of the world met to discuss its meaning. Communists and capitalists alike applauded parts of it, but each took exception to some of the points John XXIII made.

One idea the pope taught was that no person can govern others unless they want him to. Another idea was equally troubling—that ownership of goods is always limited by public need. No one has a right to own while others are in serious need.

We Americans and Europeans need to ponder what these words mean in the context of global hunger. Do we have a right to our own standard of living while millions in the Third World starve to death? Have we a right to own while little children die of malnutrition?

Do we need an international jubilee, a time of equalization, a time to put aside our weapons, a time to rest and pray?

____*Prayer*____

God of jubilees,
We need the joy and excitement of a jubilee,
    the equality and fraternity jubilee brings,
    the wholesome kindness of being equal once more.
We need to put aside
    our special titles and reserve,
    our riches and pomposity,
    our special status and regalia,
    our racial superiority
    and all the ugliness greed brings.
Send us some kind of jubilee
    in which we will be stripped down
    to the core of our goodness,
    to the heart of our lives,
    and so enjoy who and what we really are.
Lord of jubilees,
    send us jubilee now and forever.

Amen.

Prayer

God: I really have to smile at some of my children.

Me: Why, God?

God: Today I listened to a long prayer from a very good man (at least he and others hold him in high esteem). For a full 30 minutes he explained to me just what he wanted done and how to do it. He is a school principal and sounded as if he were speaking to one of his first grade students.

Me: Are you insulted, God?

God: No, no, not at all. I know my children well. I understand how nervous and even frantic they get. I realize that their hearts are in the right place, but I still have to smile—talking to God as if he were a first grader. It is no more than an occupational hazard of being principal. He talks to his wife that way, too.

Me: How should we pray, God?

God: You don't remember?

Me: What Jesus said? The Our Father?

God: That's the model. All your prayers should sound like that one. Notice that the beginning of the prayer is all about me, then it focuses on you. All prayers should have that kind of balance.

Me: I always get so interested in the me part of it that I forget to talk about you. It's not that I am selfish, God. I think, though, that I get so zeroed in on mentioning special requests that I forget that I should be saying a few nice things to you, too.

God: Please remember that. It is not that I need to hear them; you need to say them. Otherwise you make our relationship like a cafeteria. You come in and go through the line and pick out a bit of this and a bit of that. Meanwhile you forget who is providing the food.

____ *A Story* ____

Irma and Adele were college classmates. Ten years after graduation Irma happened to be in Adele's town and dropped by for a visit. Adele was surrounded by her five children, ranging in age from 8 to 2. Irma admired the children and, for a moment, wished she had had children of her own.

As the two women tried to talk, the children constantly interrupted. First it was an argument, then a need, then a hurt finger, and on and on. Adele listened patiently and solved each small problem.

Irma became tense at the constant interruptions. "How do you accomplish anything," she said, "with children pestering you all the time?"

Adele smiled. "Irma, what I accomplish each day is being in dialogue with my children. If they bring me little problems now, they will later feel free to share their real troubles with me."

God is like Adele, isn't he?

____ *Reflection* ____

One of the central teachings of the great mystics is the necessity of cultivating an awareness of the presence of God. One saint suggested that each time our hand touches a doorknob we think of God. The founder of a religious order insisted that everyone in the community stop at least once an hour to remember that God is present.

The monks of old returned to the chapel nine times each day to pray the office. People in the fields stopped their work three times a day to say the Angelus. In the early days of Christianity people turned to Jerusalem several times each day to remember the death and resurrection of Jesus.

From our tradition comes a strong urging to remember God often during each day. Is there an easier or better way to grow in holiness?

___*Prayer*___

God of compassion and tenderness,
    lover of people,
    friend of the poor,
    be my friend and love me tenderly.

Be with me every moment of my day,
    be in my sleepy eyes as I awake,
    smile at me from my morning mirror,
    share my breakfast with me, Lord.

Be with me every moment of my day,
    be on the lips of those who speak to me,
    and in my ears as I listen to them talk.

Be with me every moment of my day,
    be with me as I end this day,
    and search for sleep and quiet repose,
    be with me in my dreams both good and bad
    that I may arise eager and ready
    to spend another day with you.

Amen.

Healing

God: I am very pleased to hear people talking about healing today. I do heal and love to be asked to do it.

Me: Why do you heal some and not others, God? That has troubled me for a long time, but I have never dared to ask.

God: That is a question many of my children grapple with, and the answer is ever so simple.

Me: Simple, God? Then tell us, please.

God: I heal everyone who calls on me. No, I don't always perform what you call miracles, but I reach out with love, the greatest of all miracles, to calm and strengthen all my children.

Me: Do you mean that you heal hearts and not bodies?

God: No, I always heal hearts, and at times my healing goes beyond hearts into entire bodies. I heal memories, reconcile friends, calm fears, encourage fear-filled people, and do all those things loving parents do for their children.

Me: But why do some good people seem to suffer so much pain? It isn't fair, is it?

God: Fair is your word, not mine. I don't necessarily remove pain from those who are my best friends, but I do give them the strength to bear it. Pain has a goodness and value all its own. No one grows without pain. If I were to take away all pain, few of my children would ever grow into mature, loving, healing adults.

_____A Story_____

Bob had been a thief. He had broken into homes and stolen silverware and other valuables in order to get money for drugs. Medical help had cured him of the drug habit, but the shame of his past lived on with him.

He moved to another state and resolved never to tell anyone about his past. Then he fell in love with Ann. Should he tell her of his past? Could he let her marry him without telling her?

One evening as they sat together, Bob blurted out his story. As he spoke, beads of perspiration formed on his forehead. His hands turned cold and wet.

Ann took him into her arms and said, "Thank you, Bob, for trusting me. I love you more now than ever before."

With Ann's love, Bob could finally make peace with his past and accept himself. His healing was complete.

_____Reflection_____

For nearly a century physicians have talked about the body-soul connection in healing. They diagnose some illnesses as psychosomatic, meaning that a deep emotional problem often causes a very real bodily disorder. They have discovered that only by healing the spirit are they able to bring healing to the body.

Today, holistic medicine talks of many illnesses as functions of poor diet, lack of rest, troubled hearts and poor relationships at home.

Healing is a many-sided reality. God's healing works in ways we do not understand. Perhaps this is because we have only begun to grasp the complex relationship of body and soul. Our prayers for healing begin, or should begin, with a request that the person be healed. God knows where and how and when and why.

___*Prayer*___

God, healer of the brokenhearted,
    encourager of those twisted by pain,
    strength of the discouraged,
    power of the powerless and afraid,
    heal our pain-filled world.

Heal the insensitivity among us
    which allows Third World babies to starve
    while we labor to lose weight,
    which denies food to pregnant women
    while meeting on the right to life,
    which hoards grain in a thousand bins
    while desert tribes silently die
    because they have no food.

Heal the hardness of our hearts
    that, once healed, we may rush
    to heal our brothers and sisters
    and to create a healed world.

Amen.

Tradition

God: Are you proud of your tradition?

Me: What a funny question, God. Of course, I am proud of my tradition. Why do you ask?

God: I don't see you taking it very seriously. You seem intent on discovering new answers to all of life's questions instead of weighing the experience of your forebears. Why?

Me: God, life is new today—new questions, new problems, new technologies, new relationships. Tradition is for the museums. We are building a whole new world.

God: Ah, that is what I thought you might say. There is nothing to be learned in museums, then?

Me: Not much, God. Oh, I suppose there are a few insights but think of our world with its computers, space shuttles, television, the women's movement, nuclear power, and on and on.

God: And people?

Me: Well yes, of course, people.

God: They are still much the same, aren't they?

Me: I suppose they are, deep down inside.

God: That is why tradition is a great teacher. I don't mean that you should quit striving to improve, but I do want you to take tradition seriously as you confront your modern world. Remember, every generation thinks it is coping with a modern world. Won't your experiences have value for your children and grandchildren?

Me: I hope they will. I want to leave the world better than I found it.

God: So did your grandparents and theirs before them. Tradition is a gold mine of insight, wisdom and vitality. Use it well.

_____ *A Story* _____

A young college woman became very discouraged. Everywhere she looked she saw deception, fraud, cruelty and manipulation. One afternoon she sat in the college park and brooded. How could there be a God when the world was filled with evil?

An old nun happened by and smiled at the young woman. "Troubled, dear?" she asked.

The college woman blurted out her anger, frustration and doubt. The old nun listened.

"Let's read the first few stories in Genesis together," the nun continued. "I have a Bible with me." The girl's lips curled downward. She wanted no religious answers, no piety and certainly no retreat into the ancient Bible. However, she couldn't refuse the kindly nun.

As they read the great parable of Genesis together, the college girl began to understand how old her questions were and how writers whose names are now lost in the mists of history provided her with answers to today's problems.

Tradition is like that, present but so unobtrusive it can be missed.

_____ *Reflection* _____

History is the great liberator. When we understand the many ways our forebears have tried to cope with problems, we see how vast is our area of choice.

Without a knowledge of history, we are condemned to look at life through a narrow tunnel. We become fundamentalists under the fire of life's questions. Our fundamentalism may be the biblical variety, or it may take one of several other forms. We may be agnostic fundamentalists, liberal fundamentalists, conservative fundamentalists, and so on. What all fundamentalism has in common is an ignorance of history and tradition.

History is no dry academic discipline, then, but a storehouse of insights, values, wisdom and vitality. To be without a knowledge of history is to be condemned to repeat its mistakes and to fail to learn from its successes.

____Prayer____

God of experience and the wisdom born of it,
    you were with Abraham in his search for land,
    you blessed his children and their wives,
    you traveled to Egypt with Joseph and his brothers,
    you marched with Moses into the desert
    and stood with Joshua in the Promised Land.
Always, God, you were present,
    sharing with our forebears
    the million tiny dramas of their lives.
God of experience and the wisdom born of it,
    you were with Peter on his trip to Rome,
    you stood with Paul as he died for you,
    you lived with medieval saints and sinners,
    you helped a struggling people cope with new machines,
    and shared in the dismay of millions
    as nuclear holocaust shattered human life.
Always, God, you were present,
    sharing with our forebears
    the million tiny dramas of their lives.
Be with us today.
Awaken us to the thread of your love
    in the tradition which is ours.
Amen.

Integrity

God: Do you still believe that people's word is their bond?

Me: We don't operate that way today, God. You see, we have contracts, everything spelled out. Until you sign you haven't obligated yourself.

God: Ah, I see. You can give your word tentatively, is that it?

Me: Yes, God. We no longer live in an oral society. We write and sign everything. Fewer disputes that way.

God: That is why your courts are so full of controversies?

Me: Well, God, now that you mention it, there are many court cases. What are you driving at?

God: Very simple, really. Contracts are as good as the people who sign them. Unless these people have a basic integrity, the contracts will be violated in one way or another.

Me: Integrity. That word has a nice ring to it.

God: It is a nice word, and the reality it represents is even nicer. It means that you stand by what you promised. You may be the president of a corporation, a bishop of the church, a pastor of a parish, a storekeeper, or a traveling sales representative, but you are very disappointing in my eyes without integrity.

Me: But integrity will probably cause people to lose the advantage in dealing with others, God. They could lose money.

God: Believe me, it is better to lose money than to lose integrity. No matter how important your business may be, you are more important still and so are the people you do business with. Be honest. Maintain integrity at all costs. Let me care for the profits and losses.

____*A Story*____

Almost anyone over 50 remembers an old reading book filled with stories of integrity. One of the most endearing is about Abraham Lincoln, Honest Abe.

Early in his life Abe was a storekeeper's helper. One day, by mistake, he shortchanged an old woman. The amount was only a few cents; yet, after the long day of working the store, Abe walked miles in the snow to present the old woman the pennies that were rightfully hers.

____*Reflection*____

Management science is a good invention. It insists on clear goals and objectives, gives employees job descriptions, sets up flow charts, and assists workers in many other ways.

Yet management science, as any good student of the discipline will tell you, is no more than the form. It assumes that all people in the mix, from owner to least important employee, are honest and above-board. When this is not so, the form given by the science becomes a tool which one person can use to manipulate another.

Lack of integrity is a problem in any organization, but when that organization is one created to serve people, it is a disaster. How easy it is for administrators to convince themselves that their cause is so just that it admits of most unholy means to achieve it. Personal integrity goes a long way to limit unfair advantage and conniving at all levels.

____Prayer____

God, honest, fair and open with your people,
    awaken that same integrity in us:
    in the leaders of our nation,
    where convenience so easily wins over conscience;
    in the leaders of our businesses,
    where the bottom line of profit seems supreme;
    in the leaders of professions,
    where the client or patient is easily forgotten;
    in the leaders of our churches,
    where budgets can outweigh principle;
    in the lives we lead,
    where self can seem more important
    than all the others in the world.
God, honest, fair and open with your people,
    awaken us to integrity
    today, tomorrow and forever.

Amen.

Analogs

God: You are developing a whole new vocabulary as the computer enters your daily life.

Me: Yes, God, we are. Are there any words you particularly like?

God: I am fascinated by the word *analog*. It represents a rediscovery of an important concept.

Me: A rediscovery, God?

God: Yes, as long ago as medieval times, philosophers and theologians were fascinated by analogy. My son, Jesus, and people long before him taught in parables, a form of analogy. Only when you had your Enlightenment in the 17th century did you reject the analogy and begin to think you could say everything exactly as it was.

Me: I never knew that, God. Perhaps that explains why poets have such a hard time in today's world. They deal in analogy, don't they?

God: Yes, and it's why liturgy became so sterile. It, too, is an analogy or parable of sorts. You see one thing, but you know it means another. That willingness to live with analogy is at the root of public prayer.

Me: But why, God? Why can't our prayer be straightforward, precise and unemotional? Why does it have to be hidden in signs, symbols, melodies and rituals?

God: That is the only way public prayer can work. It must be open to the interpretations of each person present since each brings special needs, faith and problems. As long as the liturgy is open to many understandings, every need can be fulfilled and every person feel wanted and needed.

_____ *A Story* _____

Three people met in heaven one day and began to discuss the old days on earth. They wondered which of them had made the greatest contribution to human life. Eventually they went to ask Saint Peter for a final opinion.

Peter smiled at their question, knowing they must be new to heaven to be concerned about such things.

"You were a great banker," Peter began, "and you did make money available for the poor to be housed. Very good indeed."

"And you," he continued, "you were a scientist who discovered cures for a dozen diseases. Great work."

Peter gestured to the third person, saying, "And you were a bishop who led God's people into new visions of the truth. Good work too."

Then Saint Peter turned to a young woman who had tagged along to see the outcome of the debate. "But you," Peter said, "wrote songs that lifted hearts to God. You were a poet and musician. Your work will be recorded as the greatest contribution."

And, because it was heaven, everyone smiled and went back to singing God's praises.

_____ *Reflection* _____

There are, according to medieval theologians, three ways to learn—the positive way, the negative way, and the analogous way. No one can learn about God in the positive way because only God knows himself directly and immediately. We can learn about God negatively by denying any of the imperfections we see here on earth. Everything on earth ends and so by negative reasoning, we say that God is eternal, without a terminus or end.

The way we know most about God, however, is by analogy. We say God is *like* a father, *like* a mother, *like* a shepherd, and so on.

The danger with our analogies is that after a while we tend to forget that they are only analogies. We begin to think that God is *really* a human father, a mother, a shepherd—and that will not do at all.

____ *Prayer* ____

You, O Lord, are so like many things.
You are like the shepherd
    taking the smallest sheep into his arms.
You are like the thunderstorm
    full of power and eternal vigor.
You are like a father
    welcoming his errant son.
You are like a mother
    never losing faith in a wayward child.
You are like a flower
    full of beauty, color and impending joy.
You are like a melody,
    three notes in a single song.
You are like a flawless sky
    covering all things under heaven artistically.
You are like a poor man
    waiting for our widow's mite of love.
You are.
And what more can we say?
Amen.

Music

God: I heard you singing Sunday morning.

Me: What did you think, God?

God: I tried not to. Instead, I listened and enjoyed. Music is praise, and praise is to be enjoyed, not analyzed.

Me: But, God, some of our music is pretty bad. I am a folk-music fan myself. I suppose you, too, like that music best. Have you ever heard anything so boring as those 16th-century English hymns they foist off on us at our church?

God: Wait a minute. The music calls for two rest beats here. First, I am not a folk-music God. I don't like just one kind of music. I enjoy all music that comes from hearts that mean what they sing.

Me: That is the problem with some of this old music, God. I really can't mean the words, and the melodies are stale.

God: Fine, then sing your folk music, but leave room in my church for those who do not feel the same. High mass, low mass, and masses in between all please me. My love for music is really my love for the song that is in the human heart.

Me: But, God, don't you think we would be better off with just one kind of music for today's people? We used to have the Gregorian chant in the old days, remember?

God: The Gregorian chant was beautiful music, but few ever sang it. I loved to hear the refrains of "Good Night, Sweet Jesus" and

"Mother Dear, O Pray For Me" as well as the proper psalmody. It was and still is the hearts that sing. Be careful not to mix up performance with perfection. Perfect performance is often a mask providing form without reality. Relax and enjoy the music. Whatever the sound, listen for the heart. I do.

____ *A Story* ____

Once there were two great organists in a cathedral town. On Sundays they took turns playing for the high mass. Both knew their music and both played so well the huge old organ seemed to speak.

Yet the two musicians played differently. People who knew little about music felt, rather than understood, the difference. Most were drawn to the older of the two organists and did not know why.

One Sunday, after an especially dazzling performance, the younger organist went to the older and said, "I heard you play today. I could have played every note you played, but somehow my music would not be like yours. Your whole soul seems to escape into the melody."

The older man smiled an embarrassed smile and replied, "You are right. My soul is in my music, but so is yours and so, too, is the soul of every person in this church who tries to sing. As you grow older and suffer more, your soul will grow also. As it does, it will fill your music with a unique beauty all your own."

____ *Reflection* ____

Many historians tell us that the music of the Beatles was an early warning sign that ushered in a social revolution in the 1960s. These young musicians were the harbingers of one of the most profound periods of change in our era.

Other historians tell us that the change in liturgical music in the Catholic church is a sure sign that a profound change has taken place on the grassroots level of the church. It tells us that Vatican II was not, as some supposed, only a theologians' conference.

As we listen to ourselves sing, we can learn much about who and what we are and will become. The more fervently we sing, the more likely we will be to grow in love with God, even when our natural talent is quite limited.

____*Prayer*____

God of song and musical delight,
    hear our humble voices raised
    even when we cannot sing
    or understand the words we say.
God of song and musical delight,
    hear our best voices poised
    to declare in melody the thanks
    we feel and know within our hearts.
God of song and musical delight,
    hear our whistling on the way to work,
    our humming old familiar tunes,
    our cracked voices from the pews.
God of song and musical delight,
    hear beneath the faltering notes,
    beyond the flattened chords,
    and listen to our hearts
    for they are filled with a melody
    of inspired love for you.

Amen.

Sharing

God: I see you have a rack of spices in your kitchen.

Me: Yes, God. There is nothing like a touch of oregano or bay leaf to add a bit of zest to dinner.

God: Did you know that wars were fought and continents discovered in the struggle to find spices:

Me: Frankly, no, God. I didn't.

God: You have so many things you take for granted, things that in other times and places were highly prized and deeply appreciated.

Me: Such as, God?

God: Vegetables. Look at the selection in your supermarket. Fruits. Not even Solomon had so many. Salt, a prize for many ancient people. Fresh meat. Few in the world can eat as you do. Houses with roofs that keep out the elements and heating and cooling systems to make you comfortable. Window glass and cooking pots, cars and bicycles, books and even television. You have so many things.

Me: Well, yes, we do God, and we are thankful when we think about these things. It is hard to remember that all these things are gifts since we have had them all our lives.

God: Had you ever thought of sharing them with those who have so little?

Me: Please, God, all we hear these days at church is share, give, donate. Isn't there something more to religion than that?

God: Yes, there is more, of course. But all the other elements of religion have little meaning to those who will not share. Sharing is the bottom line of Christianity. If it isn't there, prayer, theology, liturgy and the rest fail to impress me.

_____*A Story*_____

The best story about gratitude concerns what happened to Jesus the day he cured the 10 lepers. He discovered that only one returned to say thank you.

An old legend has it that this Samaritan leper later welcomed the apostles to his homeland and set off with them to witness in foreign lands. He grew old and wise and a favorite of other believers for he never failed to retell the story of the day he returned to thank the Lord Jesus for his cure.

He reminded all who would listen that God's gifts all depend on gratitude. His gratitude for his cure opened him to faith, and his gratitude for faith opened him to a missionary calling, and his gratitude for that calling opened him to new friendships and great happiness.

_____*Reflection*_____

Nothing destroys a marriage like taking a partner for granted. How many wives learn to despise their husbands because these men never notice the small kindnesses offered them. How many husbands feel deep resentment toward their wives because they are never thanked for the little things like taking out the garbage.

Children easily hurt their parents by taking everything parents offer and failing to say thank you for these gifts. Friendships, too, are wrecked by lack of gratitude.

What is true in human relationships is true in our friendship with God. Because he is so kind and so generous, we can easily take his gifts for granted. When we do, we lose the wonder, the awe, and the excitement of our lives and easily pass into discontent and depression born of human greed.

_____*Prayer*_____

God of all that is or was or ever will be,
    we thank you,
    for the air around us and within us,
    for birds that fill the air with song and color,
    for the shouts of children echoing in our ears,
    for the ears to hear nature's wondrous cries,
    for the light and its sister, darkness,
    for the eyes to perceive the light,
    for lids to close our eyes for sleep,
    for the smell of meat cooking on an open fire,
    for food and warmth and wonder,
    for a world filled with gifts great and small,
    and for the variety of those gifts
        that adds spice to life
        and opens our eyes to you.

Amen.

Peacemakers

God: Did you ever think of the prophets as my outstanding peacemakers?

Me: No, God, I think of prophets as strident people, always stirring up trouble, offending important people and creating turmoil. Peacemakers are just the opposite, tranquil, gentle people who put oil on the troubled waters. How can prophets be peacemakers?

God: Was my son, Jesus, a prophet?

Me: Yes, of course.

God: Was he a peacemaker, too?

Me: Well, yes, but he was different.

God: Why was he different? He did all the things a prophet does. He announced my message and confronted evil head on, so much so that people put him to death. And he was a peacemaker, the world's greatest peacemaker at that.

Me: You have set me to thinking about peacemaking, God. Confrontation must be a part of it. I have always thought of peacemakers as quiet little people who never raised an issue and tried to avoid conflict at any price.

God: That is not peacemaking. That is cowardice. Peace lives only in an atmosphere of justice. War and turmoil continue to surface in the world's history because one group exploits another. The prophet demands that exploitation cease and so lays the groundwork for future peace.

Me: Who are the peacemakers in today's world, God?

God: They are the prophets, the men and women who insist on a redistribution of wealth in the world, who demand freedom for the oppressed, who object to exploitation of poor nations by rich ones, who demand a change of heart by rulers of nations, corporations and financial institutions. These are the peacemakers.

____A Story____

Joan and Tim were on the verge of divorce. In fact Tim had served notice that he was moving out. In desperation Joan went to a friend who commiserated with her but never challenged her. After the conversation Joan felt better, but she knew that divorce was still in her future.

That night she visited her mother and announced the news. Her mother sympathized with Joan's pain, but then confronted her by pointing out instance after instance of Joan's cruel, selfish and domineering behavior. It was a most unpleasant visit. Joan, devastated by what her mother said, left in tears.

As a result of her encounter with her mother, however, Joan took stock of her life and made up her mind to change. Today she and Tim are happily celebrating 20 years of marriage and looking back on the 15 years of joy which followed Joan's confrontation with her mother.

Who was the peacemaker, Joan's friend or Joan's mother?

____Reflection____

A surgeon who cares for his patient must often inflict pain in order to bring about a cure. A friend who loves deeply will have to confront, at times, the one loved in order to prevent disaster. Often a parent must confront a child and, at times, a child, especially an older one, may be called on to confront a parent.

Confrontation has about it an ugly ring. It is painful and unsettling, but often it is the only way to peace. If the peacemakers are the happy ones, they often purchase that happiness with the pain of confrontation, anger and hostility.

One of the paradoxes of life is the need for prophets to maintain tranquility and order.

___*Prayer*___

God of prophets old and new,
    send us prophets here today,
    for the burden of injustice
    lies heavy upon our land.
Send us prophets to proclaim
    your indignation at our callousness,
    your anger at our piled-up wealth,
    your determination to set things right,
    your hostility to injustice in our midst.
Send us prophets to insist
    that the poor have their own rights,
    that no power guarantees world peace,
    that children must not be victimized,
    that women and men are equal in your eyes,
    that the church is meant to serve.
Send us prophets, Lord,
    that we may have peace
    for only their demands for justice
    can lead us to our Promised Land.
Amen.

Freedom

God: Why do you look so troubled and confused?

Me: I've been thinking about our conversation God, and I am confused. I don't have a clear philosophy to guide me.

God: Good.

Me: But, God, that means I must make decisions on my own and be responsibile for each one of them. It means I can never relax and follow the herd.

God: Good.

Me: Life is going to be very complicated, God. Can't you help me just a little with these problems of our modern world?

God: Yes. Read the gospels and listen to the tradition of the church. But read and listen not for instant answers; rather, look for principles which you can, with fear and trepidation, apply to your modern problems. And know that I am with you and all members of the church even until the end of time.

Me: That's a comfort, God.

God: It is the best comfort I can give you. To do more would be to make you my slave, not my friend. My son, Jesus, told you that we are now friends, and being friends means we must work together to enlarge the kingdom, you and I.

_____ *A Story* _____

Lisa loved her parents deeply. In her elementary school years she was sure they had the answers for all of life's questions. Lisa brought her questions to her parents, and they provided her with answers.

In high school Lisa began to look for more than answers. She wanted values and principles to help her make her own decisions. During these years her parents spent untold hours talking about principles and teaching her by example how principles were applied to everyday problems.

As a young adult Lisa struck out on her own and began to develop her own lifestyle. She made mistakes because her understanding of her principles was faulty, and because she was not always consistent in her application of them. From each mistake, however, she learned something.

Today Lisa is a mature woman with children of her own. Now it is she who answers questions. Soon she will begin to share values and principles and, finally, watch with trepidation as her children try to apply them to their lives.

Lisa is every one of us who tries to live the gospel and pass it on.

_____ *Reflection* _____

Freedom means the ability to make choices. These choices always have their consequences. We pay for every choice we make, good and bad.

To accept the consequences of our choices is to be responsible. To try to avoid the consequences is to behave irresponsibly.

Many of us refuse to behave responsibly. We want to blame others, circumstances, history, family, economics or some force outside ourselves for the consequences of the choices we have made. The hard truth is, however, that we are free and, because we are, the consequences of our decisions belong to no one but ourselves.

——*Prayer*——

God of heaven, earth,
    and everything we have not yet imagined,
    be with me now and always.
Be with me in my struggles to understand,
    in my moments of conquest,
    in my times of awful defeat,
    in my days of exultant glory,
    in my depression and confusion, too.
Be with me, Lord, for I am yours.

Amen.